ROBERT E.
LEE
CONFEDERATE COMMANDER

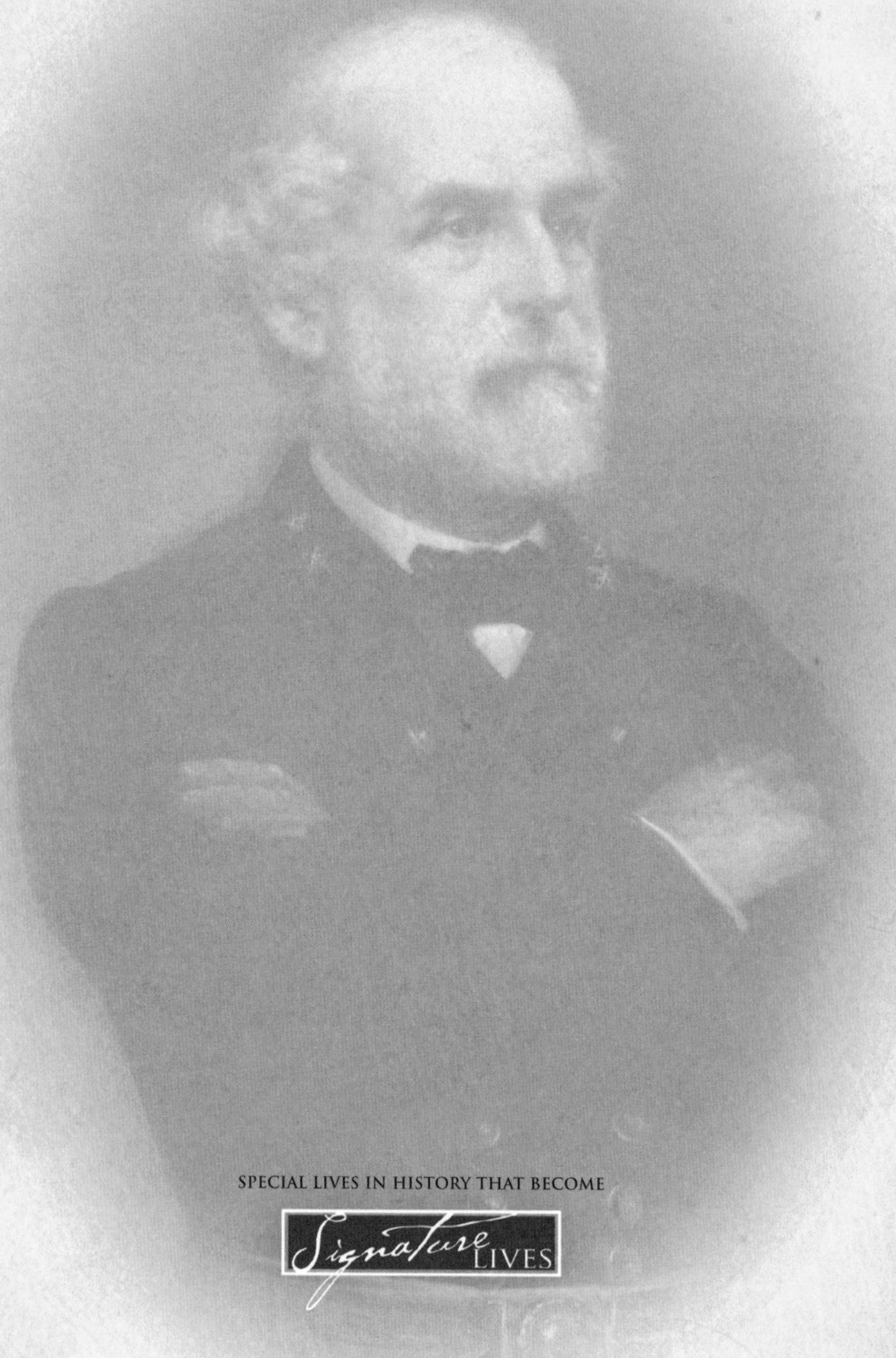

SPECIAL LIVES IN HISTORY THAT BECOME

Signature LIVES

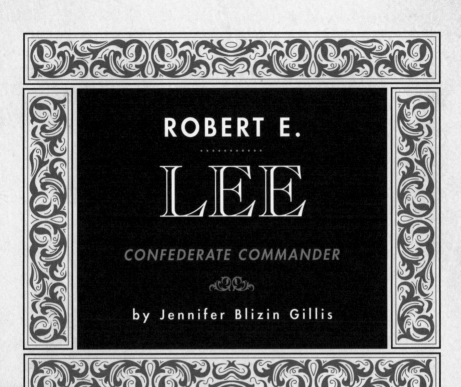

ROBERT E.
LEE
CONFEDERATE COMMANDER

by Jennifer Blizin Gillis

Content Adviser: Lisa Laskin, Ph.D.,
Lecturer on History, Harvard University

Reading Adviser: Rosemary G. Palmer, Ph.D.,
Department of Literacy, College of Education,
Boise State University

COMPASS POINT BOOKS MINNEAPOLIS, MINNESOTA

Compass Point Books
3109 West 50th Street, #115
Minneapolis, MN 55410

Visit Compass Point Books on the Internet at *www.compasspointbooks.com*
or e-mail your request to *custserv@compasspointbooks.com*

Editors: Heidi Schoof, Christianne Jones
Lead Designer: Jaime Martens
Photo Researcher: Marcie Spence
Page Production: Tom Openshaw
Cartographer: XNR Productions, Inc.
Educational Consultant: Diane Smolinski

Managing Editor: Catherine Neitge
Art Director: Keith Griffin
Production Director: Keith McCormick
Creative Director: Terri Foley

With thanks and love to Civil War buff Jerald Blizin for lively discussions
and to the belle of Front Royal, Jean Betsy Robertson, who taught me
what it means to be a Virginian - J.B.G.

Library of Congress Cataloging-in-Publication Data
Gillis, Jennifer Blizin, 1950-
Robert E. Lee : confederate commander / by Jennifer Blizin Gillis.
p. cm. — (Signature lives)
Includes bibliographical references and index.
ISBN 0-7565-0821-5 (hardcover)
1. Lee, Robert E. (Robert Edward), 1807-1870—Juvenile literature.
2. Generals—Confederate States of America—Biography—Juvenile
literature. 3. Confederate States of America. Army—Biography—Juvenile
literature. 4. United States—History—Civil War, 1861-1865—Campaigns—
Juvenile literature. I. Title. II. Series.

E467.1.L4G359 2005
973.7'3'092—dc22   2004020105

Signature Lives

CIVIL WAR ERA

The Civil War (1861-1865) split the United States into two countries and divided the people over the issue of slavery. The opposing sides—the Union in the North and the Confederacy in the South—battled each other for four long years in the deadliest American conflict ever fought. The bloody war sometimes pitted family members and friends against each other over the issues of slavery and states' rights. Some of the people who lived and served their country during the Civil War are among the nation's most beloved heroes.

Table of Contents

LEE'S STUDY

1 A Difficult Decision

❦

The evening of April 19, 1861, was a soft spring night in Arlington, Virginia. Upstairs at Arlington House, the home of Colonel Robert E. Lee, the officer paced by his desk. Lee had a big decision to make, and his decision would affect his whole life.

He had been pacing back and forth this way for hours. His morning at the War Office in Washington, D.C., seemed like a lifetime ago. The time had come for him to choose sides in the bitter Civil War that was gripping the United States. Like his home state of Virginia, Lee found himself right in the middle of the controversy about the legality of slavery. He was a career Army man, but he was used to fighting against foreign troops—not his own countrymen.

Robert E. Lee spent a lot of time writing, reading, and thinking in his study.

Lee had come back to his Arlington home that morning in a daze. With barely a word to his wife, Mary, or his children, he had gone to his room. Again and again, his thoughts returned to the morning's meetings. What was he to do? Should he take the job he was offered, or stay true to his home state?

A week before, the unthinkable had happened: Confederate soldiers from South Carolina had attacked Fort Sumter because Union soldiers were stationed there. South Carolina no longer considered itself part of the United States, and the Union soldiers were now the enemy. The newly elected president of the United States, Abraham Lincoln, was outraged. He called for 75,000 volunteers to march against South Carolina.

That very morning, Lee had met with the president's representative, Francis Blair, who said that President Lincoln wanted Lee to lead the Union against South Carolina. Lee would be promoted to general if he took command of the Army. But Lee had turned down the job.

The Lee family was considered the "royal family" of Virginia. Lees had lived at Stratford Hall, Robert's birthplace, since 1738, when the mansion was completed by Thomas Lee, who served as royal governor of the Virginia colony.

After that, he had gone to the War Office to talk things over with his old friend and

mentor, General Winfield Scott. The general felt this was Lee's big chance for honor and glory. He told Lee that he would be making the biggest mistake of his life if he turned down this chance to save his country.

The people of Charleston watched as Fort Sumter was attacked in 1861. The Civil War had begun.

But Scott did not realize the deep feelings of loyalty Lee had for his home state of Virginia. It was bad enough to take arms against South Carolina, Lee told him, but what if he should be called to take military action against Virginia? "How can I draw my sword upon Virginia, my native state?" he asked.

Just a few months before, Southern states had begun leaving, or seceding from, the United States of America. As a member of the U.S. Army, Lee had

Robert E. Lee resigned from the U.S. Army to lead Confederate troops in the Civil War.

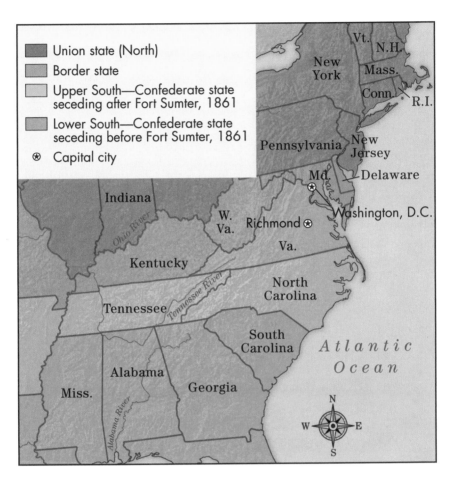

Map Legend:
- Union state (North)
- Border state
- Upper South—Confederate state seceding after Fort Sumter, 1861
- Lower South—Confederate state seceding before Fort Sumter, 1861
- ⊛ Capital city

been forced to leave Texas when that state seceded from the Union in February of 1861.

Virginia was right on the border of the North and the South.

Now Virginia's legislators were debating whether they, too, would secede. Lee had little interest in politics; in fact, he did not believe in secession. But now he realized he would have to take sides.

He had spent 36 years in the Army—but how

could he continue to serve a country that might attack his fellow Southerners? He drew strength from his sense of honor, his love for his home, and his pride in his family history. At his core, he was a Virginian first.

Some time after midnight, he stopped pacing, pulled out his chair, and sat down. He took up his pen and began to write a letter to General Scott.

Lee chose to stay true to Virginia and resigned from the U.S. Army.

Early that morning, Lee went to his wife. He showed her his letter of resignation from the U.S. Army. Lee's letter was direct:

> *"General ... Since my interview with you ... I have felt that I ought not longer to retain my commission in the Army. I therefore tender my resignation ..."*

As a result, Lee lost his U.S. citizenship and cast his fate with the Confederacy. In the days that followed, Virginia did secede from the Union. There were parties and celebrations as people caught "war fever." But not at the home of Robert and Mary Lee. A visitor there later wrote that Arlington House was like a home where there had been a death in the family. ❧

2 YOUNG ROBERT LEE

❧⁘❧

Robert Edward Lee was born January 19, 1807, at Stratford Hall on the Lee family plantation in Westmoreland County, Virginia. He was Henry and Ann Carter Lee's fifth child. The Lees were a distinguished and well-known Virginia family. Robert's father, Henry, had been a hero in the Revolutionary War. He was nicknamed "Light-Horse Harry" because of his lightning-fast raids against the British to capture supplies for George Washington's soldiers. Robert Lee's grandfather, Richard Henry Lee, had been a lawmaker who urged the colonies to become independent from Great Britain in 1776.

Robert Lee's mother, Ann, also came from a wealthy and powerful Virginia family. Her great-grandfather, Robert Carter, was called "King"

Stratford Hall is a historic landmark in Virginia today.

Henry "Light-Horse Harry" Lee was an American soldier and politician, and Robert E. Lee's father.

Carter because he owned so much land and so many slaves.

Henry Lee had been an outstanding soldier, but he was not good with money. In 1808, he lost most of his money in bad land deals. He began to write bad checks—even to George Washington—and he was sent to debtor's prison. After Henry's release from prison, the Lee family moved to Alexandria, Virginia. There, 3-year-old Robert would grow up surrounded by relatives from both sides of the family.

In 1812, Henry was involved in a political riot in Baltimore, Maryland, and was badly beaten by an angry mob. Though he recovered, his internal injuries were so severe that he was in constant pain for the rest of his life.

Because of his personal troubles and poor health, Henry decided to leave the country for the warm climate of the West Indies. He sailed to the island of Barbados in 1813, leaving his family behind. Robert was just 6 years old.

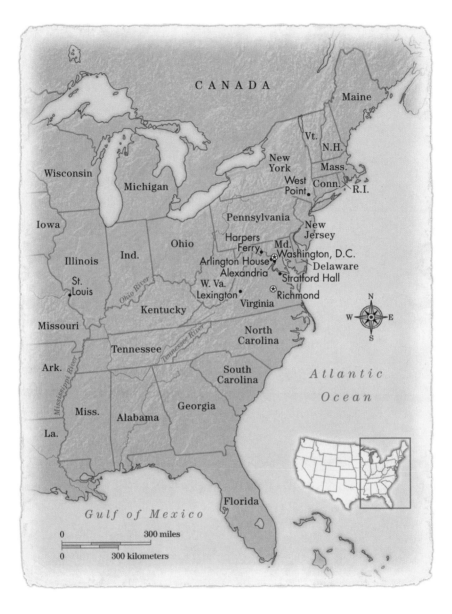

During his self-imposed exile, Henry Lee wrote letters to his family. But Robert never saw his father again. By the time Henry decided to return home, he

Robert E. Lee grew up in Virginia and later fought to defend it.

was too sick to survive the voyage. He died on March 25, 1818, at Cumberland Island, Georgia.

Ann Carter Lee, Robert's mother, was often sick and, in fact, may have had tuberculosis. Still, she maintained a home in Alexandria and raised her children with the support of numerous family members and close friends.

Cousins on the Carter side of the family numbered in the hundreds. In fact, the Carter family was so large that it had its own schools, one for girls and one for boys. When Robert was about 7, he was sent to the boys' school at Eastern View, the home of Ann's sister Elizabeth Randolph.

Ann Hill Carter Lee, the mother of Robert E. Lee

By the time he was 13, Robert was living back at home and attending the Alexandria Academy. His teacher, Mr. Leary, discovered that Robert was very good at algebra and geometry.

Robert grew very close to his mother and spent much of his time taking care of her. As the oldest son living at home, it was his job to make sure that bills were paid and servants did their jobs. Because of this, Robert was usually very serious and quiet.

Robert's mother taught her children the importance of self-control, self-denial, and the careful use of money. These qualities became the basis for Robert's fine character.

Ann Carter was also a very religious person. From her, Robert learned that complaining was not only rude, it represented a failure in trusting God. In his letters, he often wrote about things that happened as being "God's will."

Robert always wanted to please his mom. He wanted to continue his education. In those days, young gentlemen did not go into business. If they did not have money for college, they had to find a patron—someone who would pay for them to study to become a minister, doctor, or lawyer. A young man without money could also go into the military. Ann Lee had very little money. When Robert was 17 years old, he decided to apply to the U.S. Military Academy at West Point. This way, he would get a good education and become an officer in the Army. ᕲᕗ

3 THE MARBLE MAN

❦❧

Getting into West Point was not an easy task. A young man couldn't get in on good grades alone. Students had to be appointed—or chosen—by the president, after being approved by the secretary of war.

Robert E. Lee applied to War Secretary John C. Calhoun in person. He obtained letters of recommendation from certain influential relatives, his teacher, and several members of Congress. Calhoun was impressed, and Robert was officially appointed to West Point in March of 1824. Because of a very long waiting list, he didn't enter West Point until 1825.

Robert E. Lee arrived at West Point in June 1825 when he was 18 years old. School lasted for four

*Robert E. Lee was
a serious man.*

years, and there were no holidays or breaks. Students could take one eight-week vacation called a furlough, but only after they had been at West Point for two years.

For Robert, who had hardly ever been away from his family, this must have been difficult. We know it was hard for his mother. After Robert left, she supposedly said, "How can I live without Robert? He is both son and daughter to me."

The rules at West Point in the 1800s were very strict. Any cadet who was caught drinking alcohol or fighting was automatically thrown out. The students could not play cards, leave the school grounds without permission, have visitors, or read any book or magazine that was not a school assignment.

Cadets got marks against them called demerits for anything they did wrong, such as being late or not being properly dressed. Those who received too many demerits could be thrown out.

It was hard for most cadets to get through all four years without any marks against them. Robert however, did not earn a single demerit at West Point. His mother had taught him the importance of self-control, and he made her proud.

In fact, the other cadets called him "the marble man" because he looked and behaved perfectly in every situation. He was as steadfast as marble—he didn't move or crack under pressure. Like marble, Lee was also strong.

Even with his strong composure and unmoving ways, he was well-liked and friendly to everyone.

West Point has had many notable graduates. A popular expression at West Point is "much of the history we teach was made by people we taught." Confederate leaders Jefferson Davis and Thomas "Stonewall" Jackson both graduated from West Point. Presidents Ulysses S. Grant and Dwight D. Eisenhower also graduated from West Point. Women were first admitted in 1976. The academy's impressive history is one reason it's such a strong institution today.

General Joseph E. Johnston was a friend of Lee's at West Point. They later fought together for the South during the Civil War.

Classmates truly liked Lee. A classmate named Joseph E. Johnston, who later fought with Lee in the Civil War, wrote,

"No other youth ... so united the qualities that win warm friendship and command high respect. For he was full of sympathy and kindness, genial and fond of gay conversation, and even fun."

When Lee was a student at West Point, the school trained soldiers to become part of the Army Corps of Engineers. The Army Corps of Engineers began in 1775 when the Continental Congress appointed engineers to build forts at Bunker Hill, in Charlestown, Massachusetts, during the Revolutionary War (1775-1783).

In 1802, a small group of engineers was stationed at West Point, New York. These men made up the first military academy in the United States. Here, the Army Corps of Engineers began the tradition of military and civil work missions.

At West Point, it was important for the cadets to take classes in math and science and to learn about engineering so they could be part of the Army Corps of Engineers. They also took drawing classes

Today, the Army Corps of Engineers includes more than 34,000 civilians and 650 military men and women. These people work as leaders in engineering and environmental matters. They help with national security problems, national disasters, and any other national emergencies.

because engineers had to draw maps and plans for buildings. When they graduated, soldiers not only knew how to fight battles, but also how to build forts, bridges, dams, and roads to help continue building the nation.

Lee spent a lot of time on his drawings. Every detail was perfect, even though he knew the drawings would be thrown away after his teachers had graded them. He knew he would use this knowledge later in life.

Lee spent four years at the U.S. Military Academy at West Point, New York.

The skills Lee learned would eventually help him as a general during the Civil War. He knew how to organize and plan the movement of tens of thousands of troops, their weapons, and their supplies.

Lee graduated from West Point in 1829 at the age of 22 and was commissioned as a second lieutenant in the Army Corps of Engineers. He had the second-highest grades of the 46 cadets who graduated in his class. Lee was the first cadet to graduate from the academy without a single demerit.

Although Lee had graduated with high honors from West Point, he did not feel his education was complete. In fact, Lee was quoted as saying, "The education of a man is never completed until he dies."

After his graduation, Lee wanted to spend some time at home with his mother. He missed her terribly. However, Lee's excitement did not last very long. When he arrived at Ravensworth, the home of his cousins, he found his mother very sick. Lee stayed by his mother's bedside until she died. Ann Carter Hill Lee died on July 26, 1829. Lee spent the rest of that summer visiting the homes of relative and grieving for the loss of his mother. ❧

4 A Young Soldier

While visiting the homes of relatives, Lee often saw an old family friend, Mary Custis. She came from a famous Virginia family, too. Her father, George Washington Parke Custis, was the step-grandson of George Washington.

George Custis had grown up at Mount Vernon, George Washington's plantation, and was now the owner of several large plantations. The Custis family's main home was a large farm called Arlington near Washington, D.C.

In August 1829, Lee's military career outside of West Point started. During this same time, he began courting Mary. He reported to Cockspur Island near Savannah, Georgia. His job was to design and build dikes and ditches that would make the island strong

The Custis family enjoyed life at Arlington.

enough for a fort. It was not a good assignment. Storms often ruined the ditches and dikes Lee and his workers built. The heat and the mosquitoes also made the work difficult.

In 1830, Lee took a vacation to visit Mary Custis at Arlington. They became engaged and were married at Arlington on June 30, 1831.

Mary's brothers and sisters had died as infants, so she was raised an only child. She was used to getting a lot of attention and

Mary Custis Lee was an only child who was often spoiled.

having servants do everything for her. Robert, on the other hand, had grown up running his mother's house. While Robert paid attention to every tiny detail, Mary was disorganized, often late, and not a good housekeeper.

For the first three years of their marriage, Robert and Mary lived at Fort Monroe at Hampton Roads, Virginia. Their living quarters in the fort were plain and simply furnished, but the newlyweds were quite happy.

Although Mary was sick part of the time and

spent much of the winter with her parents at Arlington, Lee wrote in a letter to his good friend Jack Mackay, "I would not be unmarried for all you could offer me."

On September 16, 1832, the first of Robert and Mary Lee's seven children was born. They named him George Washington Custis Lee, after Mary's father. According to Robert, Master Custis was the most darling boy in the world.

Two years later, Lee was transferred to the position of assistant to the chief of engineers in Washington, D.C. Robert, Mary, and little Custis couldn't find a suitable house to rent in Washington, so they spent the winter of 1834 at Arlington. This arrangement suited both Mary and her parents, and Arlington became the Lee family's home for the next 30 years. Robert made the half-hour horseback ride from Arlington to his office in the capital and home again every day, unless the weather and roads were very bad.

> *Lee felt more at home at the Arlington plantation than anywhere else. The house overlooks the Potomac River and Washington, D.C. Today, the house is a memorial to Lee. It has been restored to its original state.*

In May of 1835, Lee went away to help lay out the boundary line between Michigan and Ohio. When he returned in the fall, he found Mary sick in bed at the home of relatives. After the birth of Mary Custis Lee, their second child, Mary had developed rheumatoid arthritis. Robert took his family back to Arlington and cared for his wife throughout her illness. Although his family life was very satisfying, Robert dreamed of an interesting assignment away from the office in Washington.

In April 1837, Lee was assigned to supervise an engineering project in St. Louis, Missouri. His job was to improve the harbor and make it easier for ships to travel on the upper Mississippi and Missouri rivers. On May 31, shortly before Robert left for the West, Mary gave birth to their third child, a son. They named him after Mary's uncle, William Henry Fitzhugh.

While stationed in St. Louis, Lee was homesick and lonely for his wife and children. He wrote many letters home and worried about leaving his young family without a father. In October, he wrote in a letter to his friend Jack Mackay, "I am the father of three children … so entwined around my heart that I feel them at every pulsation."

Since work on the St. Louis harbor was impossible during the winter months, Lee returned to Arlington on leave. He spent part of the winter of 1837-1838 back in the office in Washington.

That spring, Mary and the three children went with him to St. Louis. The family spent the winter

together there. Before work on the harbor began in the spring, Robert accompanied Mary and the children home to Arlington. Mary was expecting their fourth child in June.

Lee's work on the harbor made it easier for ships to get to St. Louis, Missouri.

Robert returned alone to St. Louis, where he once again wrote homesick letters to his wife:

"You do not know how much I have missed you and the children, my dear Mary. To be alone in a crowd is very solitary. In the woods I feel sympathy with the trees and birds, in whose company I take delight, but experience no pleasure in a strange crowd. I hope you are all well and will continue so, and therefore must again urge you to be very prudent and careful of those dear children."

Seven months later, Lee returned home to meet his new baby Ann Carter Lee (Annie) for the first time. Custis was 8 years old, Mary was now 6, and William (called Rooney) was almost 4. Once again, Lee returned to St. Louis alone in the spring.

On October 6, 1840, Lee completed his work in St. Louis and returned to Arlington in time for the birth of another daughter. Eleanor Agnes Lee, who was always known as Agnes, was born in early 1841.

After a few months in Washington, Lee was sent to Fort Hamilton in Brooklyn, New York. There he supervised repairs on four old forts. Since the project was scheduled to take several years, Lee was able to bring Mary and the children with him. This time, the family set up house at Fort Hamilton. They continued to

On their way to St. Louis in the spring of 1838, the Lee family shipped their furniture ahead on one steamboat and boarded another. The first boat exploded on the river and everything was lost.

George Washington Curtis Lee
1832-1913

Mary Curtis Lee
1835-1918

William Henry Fitzhugh Lee
1837-1891

Ann Carter Lee
1839-1862

Eleanor "Agnes" Lee
1841-1873

Robert Edward Lee Jr.
1843-1914

Mildred Childe Lee
1846-1905

spend their winters at Arlington, where Mary gave birth to two more children.

The seven children of Robert E. Lee as adults

Robert Edward Jr. was born in October 1843. Little Rob shared more than his father's name:

"He has a fine long nose like his father," Lee wrote to a friend in St. Louis, "but no whiskers." The final child, Mildred Childe, named after Lee's younger sister, arrived in early 1846.

Robert was not with his wife for Mildred's birth, and that winter at Fort Hamilton was one of his loneliest. His only companion was the family's little black-and-tan terrier, Spec. The Lee family was now complete.

Although Lee had risen in rank from lieutenant to captain, he was still hoping for active duty outside the Corps of Engineers. He did not want to spend the rest of his military career digging ditches and building walls. Lee's luck was about to change. By the mid-1800s, the Eastern states were crowded, and settlers were moving west. Although the government was eager to add more territory, much of the land in the West did not belong to the United States.

Lee was often lonely and greatly missed his family when he was away.

In 1845, Texas declared its independence from Mexico and became part of the United States. But

Mexico and the United States could not agree on the new border. When the Mexican army attacked a part of Texas that had been claimed by the United States, President James Polk declared war on Mexico.

In 1846, the U.S. Army sent Lee to Mexico to survey land for the commanding general, Winfield Scott. Because the Army was in Mexico, U.S. soldiers were not familiar with the land around them. Lee and other engineers located rivers and good roads, made accurate maps, and gave this information to General Scott.

General Winfield Scott was nicknamed "Old Fuss and Feathers" because of the way he looked and acted. Scott insisted on following rules perfectly. His behavior and mode of military dress carried a formal air, and he sometimes acted arrogant. Yet he could back up his arrogance. He was considered one of the most brilliant military minds of his day.

Lee often began his days at 3 a.m. and rode his horse 50 or 60 miles (80 or 96 kilometers) a day. During one battle outside Mexico City, Lee stayed awake for 36 hours straight, riding back and forth over dangerous terrain to find a way for the U.S. Army to make a surprise attack on the Mexican army. His attention to detail made him very good at mapping and describing the unfamiliar terrain.

Soon, Lee was giving General Scott advice on strategy, even though Scott was the highest-ranking officer in the U.S. Army. With Scott in command,

*The United
States and
Mexico were
fighting over
the land
between Mexico
and Texas.*

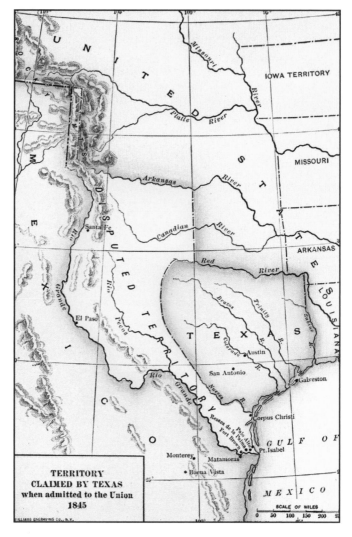

Robert and about 12,000 other soldiers took part in the battle for Veracruz, an important harbor city on the Gulf of Mexico. The American troops landed near Veracruz in March 1847 and defeated the Mexicans after a siege that lasted three weeks.

As the American troops made their way to the Mexican capital at Mexico City, Lee had the chance to put his skills to good use. The terrain included dangerous, mountainous country, but Lee's experience as an engineer helped the troops and their supplies make the journey safely. During a battle at the mountain pass of Cerro Gordo, Scott's soldiers pulled their cannons and supplies up the slopes using rope. This allowed the American troops to surprise the Mexicans by attacking them from several different directions. Lee's good work earned him promotion after promotion. As Scott's men marched toward Mexico City, Lee earned the ranks

The U.S. Navy bombarded Veracruz and took control of the Mexican War.

41

of brevet major and then brevet lieutenant. Before the Mexican War ended, he was promoted to the rank of brevet colonel. Lee was praised for his bravery and his problem-solving abilities.

A two-week break in fighting in August and September 1847 gave the Americans and the Mexicans a chance to get together and discuss terms for peace. However, when they couldn't agree to terms, the battle continued near Mexico City. After days of fierce fighting from both sides, Scott and his troops made their way into Mexico City. Though the Treaty of Guadalupe Hidalgo officially ended the war on February 2, 1848, the fighting was over after Mexico City fell to the American soldiers on September 14, 1847.

> *The human cost of the Mexican War was high. About 13,000 Mexicans and 1,200 Americans died in battle. Another 3,600 Americans and 1,300 Mexicans were wounded. Disease claimed the lives of thousands more on both sides.*

Besides making the end of the Mexican War official, the treaty also determined the border between Mexico and the United States. In the agreement, Mexico gave up nearly half of its territory, adding 525,000 square miles (1,360,000 square kilometers) to U.S. lands. Part or all of today's states of Texas, Colorado, California, Utah, Arizona, New Mexico, and Nevada became part of the United States through the Treaty of Guadalupe Hidalgo. In addition, the Rio Grande was chosen as Texas's southernmost border.

In return, the United States paid Mexico $15 million for the land and agreed to deal with any financial claims Americans made against Mexico.

The United States victory over the Mexican army taught Lee some lasting lessons. He also became a favorite of General Scott, who later wrote that Lee was "the very best soldier I ever saw in the field."

The end of the Mexican War wasn't all positive for the United States, though. Already the Northern and Southern states found themselves at odds regarding slavery. With the addition of new territory, the slavery issue rose again. Would the new states be slave or free states? It would take another war—the Civil War—to answer that question. ❧

5 TROUBLE BREWS

ಆಗ

Lee returned from Mexico hoping for more exciting assignments. Instead, he was sent to Baltimore to work on another fort. Mary and the children followed him to Baltimore, where they enjoyed a busy social life. In 1850, the Lees' oldest son, 18-year-old Custis, became a cadet at West Point. His father would soon join him there.

Because of Lee's great leadership during the Mexican War, the War Department appointed him superintendent of West Point. From 1852 to 1855, Lee ran the school he had once attended as a cadet, while his family lived in the superintendent's house. The Lees also enjoyed weekend visits from their son Custis, who was still a cadet. Lee's youngest son, Rob, who was then 10 years old, later wrote,

Lee returned to West Point as
superintendent in 1852.

"As Superintendent of the Military Academy at West Point my father had to entertain a good deal, and I remember well how handsome and grand he looked in uniform, how genial and bright, how considerate of everybody's comfort of mind and body. He was always a great favourite with the ladies ... His fine presence, his gentle, courteous manners and kindly smile put them at once at ease with him."

During his three-year stay at West Point, Lee improved the buildings and the courses offered by the school. He was a kind and fair superintendent who spent much time with the cadets and kept parents informed of how their sons were doing.

By the time Lee was 48 years old, he had spent 25 years in the Army. He was beginning to think that the rest of his military career would be spent in one boring place after another. In 1855, the Army was expanded. Lee accepted a new appointment in the cavalry. He thought he might see more action in this position. Lee became the lieutenant colonel of the 2nd Cavalry.

In the West in those days, there were often struggles between white settlers and Native Americans. The U.S. Army built forts and sent soldiers to keep the peace. In the spring of 1856, Lee was given command of Camp Cooper, an Army

An Army camp in the West

camp in Texas. He and a small group of soldiers patrolled parts of western Texas to keep the white settlers safe from attack.

Lee served with his regiment until the 1857 death of his father-in-law, George Custis, forced him to return home. In his will, George Custis left all his property to the Lee family. Lee returned to Arlington in October of 1857. Upon his return, Lee was

George Washington Parke Custis left his family with his large plantations and a lot of debt.

saddened by the condition in which he found his wife. Though she was only 49 years old, Mary was nearly crippled by arthritis. Custis had also specified in his will that his slaves be freed. At this time, slaves were seen as property. Northern states did not permit slavery, but Southern states did. Virginia was considered part of the South. Robert used his time off from the Army to see to his father-in-law's estate and take care of his wife.

On paper, George Custis had been a wealthy man. He owned at least three large plantations, including Arlington. But George Custis had not been a good manager. Some of the people he had hired to run his plantations had cheated him. He still owed money to many people. Lee had to find a way to pay off his father-in-law's debts and still keep the property his family had inherited. In order to do this, he asked for more time off from the Army to farm his father-in-law's land.

While Lee worked at Arlington in October 1859,

slavery issues between the North and the South continued to escalate. An uprising, or rebellion, at Harpers Ferry, Virginia, only made matters worse. A group of about 20 abolitionists had taken over the government arsenal there. Abolitionists were mostly Northerners who wrote books and articles about the evils of slavery, spoke against slavery, or gave money to help the antislavery cause.

John Brown was a Northern radical who, after failing at many jobs, decided to devote his life to fighting slavery. Unlike many abolitionists, Brown believed that violence was necessary to end slavery. He hoped to establish a separate state for free black people in the mountains of Virginia. John Brown thought that thousands of slaves would join his rebellion, but he could only convince a few men—black and white—to help him steal weapons from the Harpers Ferry arsenal.

John Brown's raid and stand against slavery was so famous that it became a well-known camp song. William Steffe of South Carolina wrote the song with the traditional "Glory Hallelujah" refrain. The song was especially popular among Union soldiers. They took the words to heart: "John Brown's body lies a-mouldering in the grave, but his soul goes marching on."

Once again, Lee was called to duty by the military for his leadership skills. President James Buchanan called on Lee to lead a group of Marines

John Brown on the way to his execution.

to capture the abolitionists. By the time Lee arrived, the people of Harpers Ferry had already fought with the men trying to take over the arsenal. The rebels had taken hostages and locked themselves in the firehouse. Lee sent a message to the men in the fire-house: "Surrender or be attacked." The leader of the rebellion, John Brown, refused to surrender, so Lee's Marines attacked. The hostages escaped, but some of the rebels were wounded or killed. John Brown was wounded and taken prisoner. After the rebellion failed, he was put on trial and found guilty of treason. Brown was hanged in December of 1859.

Soon after the Harpers Ferry rebellion, Lee returned to Texas with the Army. He and his soldiers continued to protect settlers from attacks by Native Americans and Mexican bandits. But Lee began to notice a change in his health. In letters to Mary, he complained of numbness and pain in his right arm. He thought he was suffering from rheumatism, but historians think he may have begun to have heart trouble. ❧

6 THE WAR BEGINS

❧❧❧

The issue of slavery had divided the United States for nearly 100 years. In 1776, the founders of the United States had argued over slavery, but decided to ignore the issue. They would let future lawmakers figure it out for themselves.

In the 1800s, there were few factories in the South. Instead, raw materials such as cotton and tobacco were grown on large plantations and then sold to Northern factories to be made into usable products. Wealthy Southern landowners used slaves to work their plantations. Southern law-makers often came from wealthy families and used their power to make sure the government protected the rights of slave owners.

The Lee family also depended on slaves to work

In the South, slaves worked in cotton fields all day.

its farms and, though Lee thought slavery was wrong, he believed it was necessary. Although more than two-thirds of the Southern population did not own slaves, their views were generally not represented in government because most Southern lawmakers owned slaves.

Slavery was not permitted in the North. With more people and bigger cities in the North, farming was not the only way to make money. People could own

Abraham Lincoln was elected president while the issue of slavery divided the nation.

businesses or work in factories. Abolitionists began demanding that slavery be declared illegal in all of the states.

As each new state joined the Union, arguments arose over whether or not slavery should be allowed there. Southern lawmakers believed that each state should have the right to make its own decisions about things like slavery. This was also called states' rights. They felt their way of life was being threatened. The slavery issue was reaching a boiling point.

In November 1860, Abraham Lincoln was elected president of the United States. Lincoln was a member of the new Republican Party, which was formed to fight the spread of slavery. Southerners were furious that a Republican had won. They felt that the North had "stolen" the election. One by one, Southern states began to break away from the United States.

In February 1861, Texas seceded from the Union. All members of the U.S. Army in Texas, including

Dates of secession for the Confederate States of America:

- South Carolina
  December 20, 1860
- Mississippi
  January 9, 1861
- Florida
  January 10, 1861
- Alabama
  January 11, 1861
- Georgia
  January 19, 1861
- Louisiana
  January 26, 1861
- Texas
  February 1, 1861
- Virginia
  April 17, 1861
- Arkansas
  May 6, 1861
- North Carolina
  May 20, 1861
- Tennessee
  June 8, 1861

The Confederate States of America elected Jefferson Davis as their president. He was inaugurated on February 18, 1861.

Lee, were ordered to leave. The Southern states decided they needed to come together. Representatives of the first seven states to secede met and voted to form the Confederate States of America. These lawmakers set up a government in Montgomery, Alabama, and chose Jefferson Davis as the president of the Confederacy.

Lee came home from Texas to a very troubled Virginia. Lawmakers there were talking about seceding, too. Lee was against secession, but he was a loyal Virginian. Although he thought that the United States should not be divided into two countries, Lee felt it was unfair for the U.S. government to tell his home state what it could or could not do.

Early in April 1861, Confederate President Jefferson Davis told President Lincoln that U.S. soldiers must leave Fort Sumter, a fort in the harbor at Charleston, South Carolina. South Carolina had been the first state to secede from the Union. Lincoln refused to order the soldiers to leave, and on April 12, the Confederate Army opened fire on the fort. These were the first shots of the Civil War.

A few days later, Lee was called to the War Office in Washington, D.C. A large army was being assembled to put an end to the Southern rebellion, and Lee was offered the command. Instead, he decided to resign from the Army. He explained this decision in a letter written after the Civil War:

> *"Though opposed to secession and depre-cating [hating] war, I could take no part in an invasion of the Southern States ... After returning to my home, I concluded that I ought no longer to retain the com-mission I held in the United States Army ... At the time, I hoped that peace would have been preserved; that some way would have been found to save the country from ... war; and I then had no other intention than to pass the remainder of my life as a private citizen."*

On April 17, 1861, Virginia's lawmakers voted to secede from the Union and join the Confederate States of America. Lee was asked to join the Confederate cause. Though he had never really commanded soldiers in battle, Robert E. Lee was

Lee dressed in his full Confederate military uniforn

given the rank of major general in the new Confederate military and made commander of the Virginia military and naval forces. His experience as West Point superintendent was paying off. Lee had to work very quickly to get supplies, food, and soldiers for the new army.

Walter Taylor worked with Lee at this time. In his journal, Taylor described Robert E. Lee in 1861:

> *"Admirably proportioned, of graceful and dignified carriage, with strikingly handsome features, bright and penetrating eyes, his iron-gray hair closely cut, his face cleanly shaved except a moustache, he appeared every inch a soldier and a man born to command."*

Lee warned his fellow Virginians that it would be a long and bloody war. He knew his tiny army only had 60,000 guns and 200 kegs of powder. It was not a very promising beginning. The Union Army was much better prepared and had more resources. Lee would also be leading his troops against his former commander during the Mexican War, Winfield Scott.

THE ARMY OF NORTHERN VIRGINIA

Chapter

7

ᥬᥬᥬ

In May 1861, the Confederate States of America moved its capital to Richmond, Virginia. Lee's newly organized Virginia troops became part of the regular Confederate Army. The Confederate Army did not have a general-in-chief over all its forces. Instead, Confederate President Jefferson Davis was in charge of several armies, or groups of soldiers, all under the command of different generals. Most of them argued with each other and with Davis about how to conduct the war.

The first big battle of the Civil War took place in July 1861 at the small town of Manassas, between Washington, D.C., and Richmond. It is known as the First Battle of Bull Run. Although the Union Army was bigger and better prepared, the Confederate

Although the Confederate Army was smaller, it fought with great spirit.

Rebels trained hard and were willing to fight.

Army won the battle. Some Confederate soldiers even thought that the war was over, and they left for home when the fighting ended. But there were many more battles to come.

That fall, Davis sent Lee to western Virginia to make sure that Union soldiers did not get through the mountains to attack Richmond. There was fighting, but no one seemed to be losing or winning. Many Confederate soldiers got sick and died from the cold, wet weather.

Lee knew that the Confederate Army had a better chance of winning if they waited for the

Union Army to attack first. Newspapers accused him of avoiding fights and called him "Granny Lee." Jefferson Davis, however, had so much faith in Lee that he made him a full general in the Confederate Army and put him in charge of defending the South Carolina coast. Like his service in Mexico, this coastal command gave Lee valuable experience in several areas. He learned about managing larger groups of men. He studied the railroads—how best to use them to move troops and also how best to defend them. Finally, it strengthened his belief in the use of earthworks—ditches and dirt walls that were built to improve the army's position on the battlefield.

Earthworks had not been used much in the

General Robert E. Lee (center) meets with Confederate President Jefferson Davis (fourth from left) and his Cabinet.

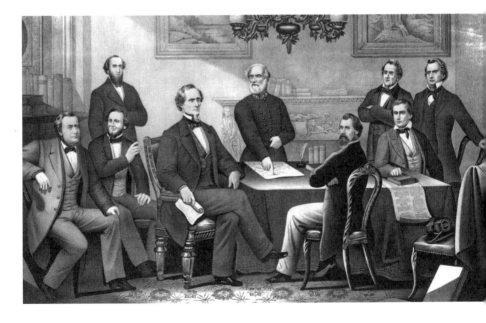

United States before the Civil War, and orders to "dig in" brought much grumbling from the men. Lee soon earned the nickname "The King of Spades" for all the digging he made his men do. Confederate volunteers considered digging to be "labor no white man should do." Many also felt that Southerners were too brave and too proud to hide behind dirt.

When he returned to Richmond in March of 1862, Lee continued to serve as a valuable military adviser to Jefferson Davis. He helped to draw up plans for General Joseph E. Johnston's troops in Virginia. Lee knew what the Confederacy was facing. He knew that the Union Army was bigger, better equipped, and better trained than the Confederate Army.

> *Jefferson Davis trusted Lee, but also took advantage of him. Davis used Lee as his secretary of war without giving him the title, the pay, or the power of the office.*

On May 31, 1862, Confederate General Joe Johnston was wounded in the Battle of Fair Oaks (also known as Seven Pines). The next day, Jefferson Davis put Lee back in charge of the Virginia forces. Lee renamed the soldiers fighting under him the Army of Northern Virginia. By the time Lee took command, Union soldiers under General George McClellan had pushed their way to within 7 miles (11 kilometers) of Richmond.

In a series of battles known as the Seven Days, Lee forced the retreat of General McClellan and his Union troops from the Richmond area. Lee soon began to show his military genius. He seemed to figure out what the Union generals were going to do and then beat them to it. His officers were always in the right place at the right time. The Army of Northern Virginia won battle after battle. Luck was definitely on Lee's side.

Lee was lucky to have excellent generals and officers, some of whom had also gone to West Point. He thought it was important to trust his officers' decisions. If one of his generals felt strongly about doing something a certain way, Lee would agree. This worked well for the first two years of his command. It also helped that the Union generals were too cautious, pulling back and reorganizing their soldiers instead of attacking when the Confederates were weakest. This gave Lee time to move his few soldiers around and plan the next battle.

Confederate General Thomas Jackson was nicknamed "Stonewall" for his firm determination in battle.

Lee counted on two of his most trusted officers, James Ewell Brown "Jeb" Stuart and Thomas "Stonewall" Jackson, to keep the Confederates one step ahead of the Union Army. His strategy was an "offensive defense"—he did not believe in waiting for his enemies to attack him. First, he would send the cavalry under Stuart to study the countryside and find out where the Union soldiers were. In a few battles, Lee would divide his army and send half of his men with General Stonewall Jackson to attack from one side while he attacked from the other.

Like Lee, both Stuart and Jackson were Virginians and graduates of West Point. Stuart, the commander of Lee's cavalry, was known for his enormous beard and his fondness for uniforms that included red capes and feathered hats.

Thomas "Stonewall" Jackson was a professor at Virginia Military Institute in Lexington when the Civil War began. He earned his nickname at the first battle of Manassas: When he was told that Union soldiers were breaking through the Confederate line, Jackson calmly replied that his soldiers would be stronger than them. One soldier said that Jackson stood there like a stone wall.

As the Union Army retreated after the series of battles known as the Seven Days, Lee decided to lure them farther away from Richmond by moving

Conferate General James "Jeb" Stuart fought at the Battle of Bull Run and the Battle of Fredericksburg.

his troops west and north into Maryland. There he hoped to fight a major battle that would bring a clear victory to the Confederates.

In August, the Confederates fought—and won again—at Manassas. By early September, Lee had moved into Maryland with about 40,000 soldiers. On September 17, 1862, they faced a Union Army of about 72,000 soldiers near the town of Sharpsburg, Maryland, on the Antietam River. After a single, terrible day of fighting, called the Battle of Antietam, 13,000 Union soldiers were dead or missing. Lee had lost 10,000 soldiers—one-fourth of his Army of Northern Virginia. The Confederates were forced to retreat into Virginia.

The Battle of Antietam left thousands of soldiers dead.

After only one year of war, the Confederate States of America was already desperate. The North had more soldiers, more money, and more factories to make weapons and supplies for its army. The Confederacy was barely able to keep its soldiers fed and clothed. In a letter to Jefferson Davis in 1862, Lee wrote:

The Battle of Antietam in Maryland on September 17, 1862, remains the bloodiest day in American history. Nearly 23,000 soldiers died.

"The army ... lacks much of the material of war, is feeble in transportation, the animals being much reduced, and the men are poorly provided with clothes, and in thousands of instances are destitute of shoes."

Although his soldiers were hungry, Lee tried to keep them from stealing anything. The army was supposed to buy its food from local farmers, but in many cases the food was just taken—this was called impressment. The farmers were given a receipt, which they were supposed to take to a government clerk to be paid in Confederate dollars. But Confederate money was quickly becoming worthless, so the farmers lost money on the deal. They were not happy about food being taken from them.

One story about Lee says that he surprised a

Lee used this house as his military headquarters during the Battle of Gettysburg.

Confederate soldier who had just stolen a pig from a nearby farm. Lee was furious and ordered other soldiers to arrest the man so he could be tried and executed. Instead, as punishment, the thief was sent to the front lines.

It was common at this time for officers to take over private homes as their headquarters. Lee, however, insisted on living in a tent. On the rare times that he did stay in someone's house, he insisted on taking the smallest room.

Lee was with his army at Culpeper Court House, Virginia, in October 1862 when he got word that his 23-year-old daughter, Annie, had died of typhoid fever. Robert Lee had seen little of his wife and children since the war began in 1861. Lee wrote to his wife,

> *"I wish I could give you any comfort, but beyond our hope in the great mercy of God, and the belief that he takes her at the time and place when it is best for her to go, there is none."*

Arlington, the Lee's home, had been captured in the first days of the Civil War. Mary had moved from house to house, finally ending up in a rented house in Richmond. Since Mary was becoming more and more crippled by her arthritis, her daughter Agnes stayed home to take care of her. Custis, the oldest son, had become part of Jefferson Davis's staff. Rooney had been promoted to brigadier general, and Rob Jr. had left the University of Virginia to enlist in an artillery unit. Mary, the oldest daughter, was staying with friends, and Mildred, now 16, was in boarding school in Raleigh, North Carolina. ❧

8 A TURNING TIDE

Chapter

❧◆❧

In November 1862, the Union Army and Lee's Army of Northern Virginia faced off at Fredericksburg, Virginia, in one of the bloodiest battles of the Civil War. From a favorable position on Marye's Heights, Lee's army mowed down wave after wave of Union soldiers—14 units in all—who were forced to fight uphill. One survivor was reported as saying, "We might as well have tried to take hell."

During the Battle of Fredericksburg, it is said that Lee turned to one of his generals and said, "It is well that war is so terrible. We should grow too fond of it."

After the deadly defeat at Fredericksburg, the Union Army under General Ambrose E. Burnside retreated across the Rappahannock River.

Confederate troops fight from behind a stone wall at Fredericksburg.

Winter set in after the battle at Fredericksburg. The Union and Confederate Armies spent one of the coldest winters on record camped across the Rappahannock from each other. Lee wrote to his wife, Mary, that the snow was up to his knees and the soldiers had little food. To make matters worse, Lee became very ill with a cough and fever, along with pain in his chest, back, and arms. Although he once again blamed his pains on rheumatism, his heart problems were probably getting worse.

The fighting began again in the spring of 1863 with the Battle of Chancellorsville in Virginia. Lee had managed to build his army back up to about 78,000 soldiers. Despite his troops being tired and hungry, Lee was winning battles. Reporters came to the field to interview him. Southern ladies sent him picnic baskets of food. But Lee refused to take any credit—he believed everything that happened was part of God's plan.

General Ambrose E. Burnside, the general who fought against Lee at Fredericksburg, had some really strange facial hair on either side of his head, which soon was imitated by other men, and became known as "sideburns."

In May, Confederate General Stonewall Jackson was wounded by "friendly fire" at Chancellorsville, when his own men mistook him for a Union soldier. When Lee was told that Jackson's left arm had to be amputated and that he was near death, he said,

"He [Jackson] has lost his left arm, but I have lost my right arm!" He meant that Stonewall Jackson was his "right-hand man," the person he most depended upon.

Although the Battle of Chancellorsville was a Southern victory, Jackson's death was disastrous for the Confederate Army. Lee and Jackson had been an unbeatable team. They understood each other completely.

Confederate Generals Stonewall Jackson (left) and Robert E. Lee meet in 1863 for the last time before Jackson is shot and killed.

75

Now more than ever, Lee believed that he had to face the Union Army in one decisive battle. His army didn't have the strength to fight much longer, especially without Stonewall Jackson. Then, he hoped, the North would make a peace agreement with the South and end the Civil War. His hungry, ragged army was getting weaker. Lee marched his troops into Pennsylvania, hoping to find enough food for them in the rich farmland there.

In June 1862, Lee sent General Stuart and his cavalry to find out where Union General McClellan's troops were. With his soldiers, Stuart rode completely around the Union Army, capturing a supply train and 165 Union soldiers before returning to Lee with his report.

By July 1863, Lee's troops had reached southern Pennsylvania. They were stopped at the town of Gettysburg by the Union Army of Major General George G. Meade. Fighting broke out between groups of Confederate and Union soldiers on July 1. Union soldiers moved to the tops of three hills: Culp's Hill, Cemetery Ridge, and Little Round Top. Without the much-needed land surveying of Stuart, Lee was not able to organize his army in time to take the high ground for himself. He knew this was going to be a deadly fight.

On July 3, Confederate soldiers under the command of General George Pickett charged uphill

Thousands of soldiers were fatally wounded during the Battle of Gettysburg in 1863.

against Union artillery and were mowed down by cannon fire. Afterward, Lee is said to have ridden along the lines claiming, "All this has been my fault." Many historians think that the Confederacy lost the war that very day.

After the Battle of Gettysburg, 28,000 of the 75,000 Confederate soldiers were dead, wounded, or missing. Union casualties were 23,000 out of 83,000 men. The Army of Northern Virginia retreated to its home state. The three-day battle was memorialized by Abraham Lincoln in his "Gettysburg Address of 1863," which honored the battle's fallen soldiers.

Almost overnight, Lee's popularity vanished. Newspaper articles called Lee's plans to invade Pennsylvania foolish. The press blamed him for losing at Gettysburg. Since the spring of 1863, Lee's health had been failing. Now he wrote a letter to Jefferson Davis offering to resign, saying,

General Robert E. Lee, 1865

"[I believe] that a younger and abler man than myself can readily be obtained." Lee went on to say that it would be the happiest day of his life to see at the head of the Confederate Army "a worthy leader—one that would accomplish more than I could perform and all that I have wished."

Davis replied, "Our country could not bear to lose you." He wrote that it would be impossible to find someone better suited to the command than Robert E. Lee.

In December 1863, Lee made a rare visit to his home in Richmond, where he found Mary totally confined to a wheelchair. His son Rooney had been captured and imprisoned at Fort Monroe in Virginia, and then moved to Fort Lafayette in New York. Rooney's wife, Charlotte, was seriously ill, and her health was made worse by her worry over her husband. She died later that month. Since the Lee family was unable to pay the property taxes on Arlington in person, as required by a new law, the United States government was preparing to take it away from them.

When the Lee family couldn't pay their taxes, their Arlington plantation home was taken by the federal government. It was used as a military headquarters. Today, the mansion that was built by George Washington's adopted grandson to honor Washington stands as a memorial to Robert E. Lee. It overlooks Arlington National Cemetery in Virginia.

Union General Ulysses S. Grant stands outside his tent at his head-quarters in City Point, Virginia.

As 1864 began, there was no good news for the Lee family. There was also little good news for the Confederacy. Confederate armies had been defeated in South Carolina, Georgia, Mississippi, and Tennessee.

In March of 1864, President Lincoln put General Ulysses S. Grant in charge of the entire Union Army. There would be no more lucky breaks for Lee.

General Grant planned a huge, coordinated offensive involving all of the armies of the United States. While Union General William T. Sherman went after the city of Atlanta, Grant took on Lee's Army of Northern Virginia.

In battle after battle, Grant's forces pushed the Confederate Army back toward Richmond. By fall 1864, the two armies were simply shooting at each other from trenches all around Petersburg, Virginia. Lee knew that it would only be a matter of time before his army ran out of food.

Late in March 1865, Lee decided to make a last

attempt to bring the siege to an end. He attacked a Union fort near Petersburg, but his soldiers were quickly overrun by Union troops. On April 2, Grant's army broke through the Petersburg defenses. Lee's

Most battles of the Civil War were fought in the South.

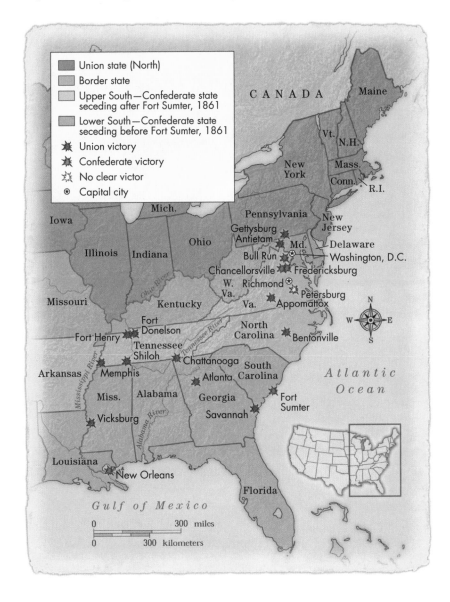

Union state (North)
Border state
Upper South—Confederate state seceding after Fort Sumter, 1861
Lower South—Confederate state seceding before Fort Sumter, 1861
Union victory
Confederate victory
No clear victor
Capital city

CANADA   Maine

Vt. N.H.

New York   Mass.

Conn. R.I.

Iowa

Mich.

Pennsylvania New Jersey

Gettysburg
Antietam   Md.   Delaware

Illinois   Indiana   Ohio

Bull Run   Washington, D.C.

Chancellorsville   Fredericksburg

W. Richmond
Va.   Petersburg

Missouri

Kentucky   Va.   Appomattox

Fort
Donelson   North
Carolina   Bentonville

Fort Henry

Tennessee

Shiloh   Chattanooga   South
Carolina

Arkansas   Memphis   Atlanta

Miss.   Alabama   Georgia   Fort
Sumter

Vicksburg   Savannah

*Atlantic
Ocean*

Louisiana

New Orleans

Florida

Gulf of Mexico

0   300 miles

0   300 kilometers

Thousands of Confederate soldiers lost their lives on Civil War battlefields.

ragged army was forced to abandon the city of Richmond. As the Army of Northern Virginia retreated southward, the Union Army chased it in a series of running battles.

Lee hoped to join General Joseph Johnston's army in North Carolina, but his troops were cut off and surrounded by Union forces at the village of Appomattox Court House, Virginia.

Then Lee received a letter from General Grant,

Robert E. Lee and Ulysses S. Grant corresponded with each other before the official surrender.

SURRENDER OF Gen. LEE,

AND THE ARMY OF NORTHERN VIRGINIA

WAR DEPARTMENT, April 9, 1865.

GENERAL STEVENSON:

This Department has just received the official report of the surrender of General Lee and his army to Lieut. General Grant, on the terms proposed by General Grant. Details will be given as speedily as possible.   E. M. STANTON.

HEADQUARTERS ARMIES OF THE UNITED STATES,

To E. M. STANTON, Secretary of War.   4:30, P. M., April 9, 1865.

General Lee surrendered the Army of Northern Virginia, this afternoon, upon terms proposed by myself. The accompanying additional correspondence will show the conditions fully.   U. S. GRANT, Lieutenant General.

GENERAL,   April 9, 1865.

I received your note of this morning on the picket line, where I had come to meet you and ascertain definitely what terms were embraced in your proposal of yesterday with reference to the surrender of this army. I now request an interview in accordance with the offer contained in your letter of yesterday, for that purpose.

Very respectfully, your obedient servant,

To Lt. Gen. U. S. GRANT, Com'd'g U. S. Armies.   R. E. LEE, General.

General R. E. LEE, Com'dg C. S. Armies.   April 9, 1865.

Your note of this date is but this moment (11.50, A. M.) received, in consequence of my having passed from the Richmond and Lynchburg road to the Farmville and Lynchburg road. I am, at this time, waiting about four miles west of Waller's Church, and will push forward to the front for the purpose of meeting you. Notice sent to me on this road, where you wish the interview to take place, will meet me.   Very respectfully, your obedient servant,   U. S. GRANT, Lieut. General

APPOMATTOX COURT HOUSE, April 9, 1865.

General R. E. LEE, Commanding C. S. A.

In accordance with the substance of my letter through you, of the 8th inst., I propose to receive the surrender of the Army of Northern Virginia, on the following terms, to wit : Rolls of all officers and men, to be made in duplicate, one copy to be given to an officer designated by me, the other to be retained by such officer or officers as you may designate. The officers to give their individual parole not to take arms against the Government of the United States, until properly exchanged ; and each Company or Regimental Commander sign a parole for the men of their command. The Arms, Artillery and public property to be parked and stacked, and turned over to the officers appointed by me to receive them. This will not embrace the side-arms of the officers, nor their private horses or baggage. This done, each officer and man will be allowed to return to their homes, not to be disturbed by United States authority so long as they observe their parole and the laws in force where they may reside.   Very respectfully, your obedient servant,   U. S. GRANT, Lieut. General.

HEADQUARTERS ARMY OF NORTHERN VIRGINIA,

To Lieut. General U. S. GRANT, Commanding.   April 9, 1865.

General —I have received your letter of this date, containing the terms of surrender of the Army of Northern Virginia, as proposed by you ; as they are substantially the same as those expressed in your letter of 8th inst., they are accepted. I will proceed to designate the proper officer to carry the stipulations into effect.   Very respectfully, your obedient servant,   R. E. LEE, General.

asking him to surrender. Lee had little choice. His troops were exhausted, starving, and didn't have any supplies. Lee wrote back to Grant asking for the terms of the surrender.

9

EVEN IN DEFEAT—A HERO

෴

On April 9, 1865, Robert E. Lee and Ulysses S. Grant met at the Appomattox home of Wilmer and Virginia McLean. General Grant had a deep respect for the older Robert E. Lee, and he tried to make the surrender as easy as possible. The terms, written by Grant and approved by Lee, allowed the Confederate troops to take their horses home for spring plowing. The Union Army also agreed to provide 25,000 rations to feed the starving Confederate soldiers.

As Lee left the McLean house and mounted his horse, Grant and his officers removed their hats in a show of honor and respect. Lee then returned through the lines of his soldiers on his beloved horse, Traveller. As his army crowded around him,

Ulysses S. Grant (left) and Robert E. Lee met to discuss the terms of Lee's surrender.

Lee leaving the McLean home after his surrender.

he choked back tears, saying: "Men, we have fought through the war together. I have done my best for you; my heart is too full to say more."

Lee stayed with the Confederate soldiers as they stacked their weapons outside Appomattox Court House. Then he climbed on Traveller and rode to

Richmond. During the Civil War, Lee had begun as an unpopular figure, gained great popularity, and then lost it again. Now, as his army surrendered, he was a hero. As he rode into Richmond, crowds followed him to the doorstep of his house. Instead of making a speech, he simply went into the house and closed the door. His son Rob later wrote that if his father wanted to go for a walk, he had to do it at night. Otherwise, he was overwhelmed by crowds of people who wanted to talk to him.

Lee and Grant had agreed that the Confederate soldiers who surrendered at Appomattox could all go home free men. As long as they promised never to fight against the Union again, even officers could go

General Robert E. Lee's hat, binoculars, belt, and 1851 Colt Navy .36 revolver

free. However, when President Lincoln was assassinated just a few days after Appomattox, angry Northerners demanded that the South be punished for its part in the Civil War.

The new president, Andrew Johnson, planned to put anyone who had been part of the Confederate government on trial for treason. Jefferson Davis was arrested and thrown into prison. Lee worried that he would be arrested, too. But Grant insisted that Lee had promised never to fight again. Grant convinced President Johnson not to put Lee on trial.

Lee had hoped to retire and write a history of the war in Virginia. He thought about buying some land and farming, as his sons Rooney and Rob were doing. But in August 1865, the board of trustees of Washington College chose him to become the college president. They offered him $1,500 a year, a home, and a percentage of the tuition each student paid to go to school there. In September, Lee rode Traveller to Lexington, Virginia, where the college was located.

Like many places in southern Virginia, the college had been heavily damaged during the Civil

When Robert E. Lee applied for citizenship, his signed oath of allegiance was somehow misplaced. The missing paper was found in 1970 by an employee of the National Archives. Lee's full U.S. citizenship was restored by an act of Congress in 1975.

War. Only five professors and fewer than 50 students remained. The trustees hoped that Lee's fame would attract more students to the school.

Lee's presence did even more for the school than

Washington and Lee University included the name of its former president, Robert E. Lee, in 1870.

89

the trustees expected. More students did come, and Lee worked with a committee to add new buildings, including a chapel and a new house for himself and his wife. He added more classes and made the small college into a modern university. He personally met with students who were not doing well in school and often wrote to their parents to let them know how they were doing.

Though Lee enjoyed his work at the school, his health was failing. In 1870, he wrote his daughter Mildred that he could not walk uphill without sitting down for a rest. He often suffered from chest pains. Mary Lee wrote that he moved stiffly and that his face looked red much of the time. He was seeing two doctors, but in those days no one knew very much about heart disease. They told Lee to get more rest and to drink lemon juice.

Some Southerners wanted to keep their anger and bitterness alive. When they looked to Lee to be their leader, he shook his head at them. "Abandon your animosities," he said, "and make your sons Americans."

The professors at the college voted for Lee to take a vacation. Throughout the spring and summer of 1870, he made several trips. He took a "farewell tour" of several Southern states with his daughter Agnes. Then he spent time visiting close friends and family. Lee knew that his health was failing.

When fall came, Lee went back to work as president of Washington College. One rainy afternoon in late September, he went to a church meeting that lasted until 7 p.m. He came home to find the family gathered around the dinner table. Lee then went to his place at the table and seemed as though he were going to say grace. But he was not able to speak and quickly sat down.

His family realized that something was wrong. By the time his doctors got there, Lee could not speak clearly. They put him to bed and for a few days he seemed to improve a little, though he still could not speak. He knew he was dying. When

Lee's family stayed next to his bed during his final days.

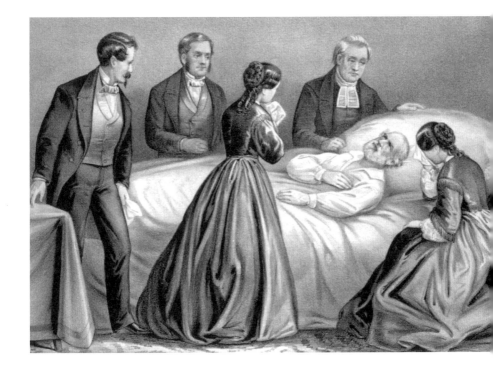

someone joked that he needed to get up and ride Traveller, he shook his head and looked up toward the ceiling.

For two weeks, Lee lay in bed. His family and doctors hovered around, hoping he would get better or say something. Robert E. Lee died on October 12,

A large monument honors Robert E. Lee in the Lee Chapel at the Washington and Lee University in Lexington, Virginia.

1870, and was buried in Lexington, Virginia, in the Chapel at Washington College. Lee's beloved horse, Traveller, walked behind Lee's hearse in the funeral procession. When Traveller died the next year, he was buried just outside the entrance to the chapel where Lee's body rests. This chapel is sometimes called "The Shrine of the South" and is visited by thousands of people every year.

Although Lee did not believe the United States should ever be divided into two separate countries, he supported and fought for the Confederacy because of an unshakable loyalty to his home state of Virginia. He fought not for personal gain, but to prove himself worthy of a cause.

At the same time, a part of this cause was to protect slavery. No matter how great a man Lee was, he still believed that some people weren't created equal. In the view of many Americans today, this is a major flaw in a man who was other-wise considered remarkable.

However, Lee was idolized by his soldiers and won the admiration and respect of nearly all Southerners. Many historians think of him as a military genius. Despite overwhelming odds, Lee managed to keep the Confederacy alive for four years with a small force of soldiers who were underfed and poorly armed. Other historians think Lee was a bad general who saw

Lee on his famous horse, Traveller

thousands of casualties in the face of increasingly desperate odds.

After the Civil War, Jefferson Davis, the president of the Confederacy, was put in prison. But Robert E. Lee, commander of the Confederacy's soldiers, went free. Although the South lost the Civil

War, Lee urged Southerners to accept the outcome and move forward. His attitude was very important at a time when many felt only bitterness and hatred.

More than one hundred years later, people still argue about the Civil War. To many, Lee is a Civil War hero. To others, Lee was another slave-owner who led the fight to preserve slavery in the Southern states. No matter what you believe, Robert E. Lee will always be an important part of the Civil War and the history of the United States.

In the end, the man who had fought against the Union showed the world how to work peacefully and honorably for a country that was united once again. ✑

LEE'S LIFE

1825

Lee enters U.S.
Military Academy
at West Point

1807

January 19, Robert E.
Lee is born at
Stratford, Virginia

1818

Lee's father dies

1810

1809

Louis Braille of
France, inventor of a
writing system for the
blind, is born

1821

Central American
countries gain
independence
from Spain

1826

The first photo-
graph is taken by
Joseph Niépce, a
French physicist

WORLD EVENTS

1829

Graduates from
West Point; Lee's
mother dies

1830

First assignment,
Army Corps of
Engineers

1831

Marries Mary Ann
Randolph Custis
at Arlington, her
family home

1830

1829

The first practical
sewing machine is
invented by French
tailor Barthélemy
Thimonnier

1833

Great Britain
abolishes slavery

LEE'S LIFE

1837

Lee is sent to St. Louis, Missouri, as part of U.S. Army Corps of Engineers

1846

Serves in Mexican War, performs land surveying for General Winfield Scott

1852

Appointed superintendent of West Point, serves three years

1850

1836

Texans defeat Mexican troops at San Jacinto after a deadly battle at the Alamo

1846

Irish potato famine reaches its worst

1848

The Communist Manifesto by German writer Karl Marx is widely distributed

WORLD EVENTS

1859

Helps put down John Brown's rebellion at Harpers Ferry, Virginia

1861

April 12, Confederate soldiers fire at Fort Sumter, South Carolina, starting the Civil War; Lee resigns from the U.S. Army; Virginia secedes; Lee appointed head of Virginia army

1856

Lee transfers to the cavalry and serves in Texas

1860

1858

English scientist Charles Darwin presents his theory of evolution

1860

Austrian composer Gustav Mahler is born in Kalischt (now in Austria)

LEE'S LIFE

1862

Lee appointed commander of Army of Northern Virginia

1863

May 10, Lee's "right-hand man" Stonewall Jackson dies of wounds from Battle at Chancellorsville; Lee's army defeated at Gettysburg

1862

Victor Hugo publishes *Les Misérables*

1863

Thomas Nast draws the modern Santa Claus for *Harper's Weekly,* although Santa existed previously

WORLD EVENTS

1865

April 9, Lee surrenders to U.S. Grant at Appomattox Courthouse, Virginia; Lee becomes president of Washington College, Lexington, Virginia; Applies for pardon from U.S. government (application lost)

1870

October 12, Lee dies at Lexington

1865

1870

1869

The periodic table of elements is invented by Dimitri Mendeleyev

1865

Lewis Carroll writes *Alice's Adventures in Wonderland*

DATE OF BIRTH: January 19, 1807

BIRTHPLACE: Stratford Hall Plantation, Westmoreland County, Virginia

FATHER: Henry "Light-Horse Harry" Lee III (1756-1818)

MOTHER: Ann Hill "Nancy" Carter Lee (1773-1829)

EDUCATION: U.S. Military Academy, West Point

SPOUSE: Mary Anna Randolph Custis Lee (1808-1873)

DATE OF MARRIAGE: June 30, 1831

CHILDREN: George Washington Custis Lee (1832-1913)
Mary Custis Lee (1835-1918)
William Henry "Rooney" Fitzhugh Lee (1837-1891)
Ann Carter Lee(1839-1862)
Eleanor "Agnes" Lee (1841-1873)
Robert Edward Lee Jr. (1843-1914)
Mildred Childe Lee (1846-1905)

DATE OF DEATH: October 12, 1870

PLACE OF BURIAL: Chapel, Washington College (now Washington and Lee University), Lexington, Virginia

In the Library

Anderson, Paul Christopher. *Robert E. Lee: Legendary Commander of the Confederacy.* New York: PowerPlus Books, 2003.

Ashby, Ruth. *Lee vs. Grant: Great Battles of the Civil War.* Mankato, Minn.: Smart Apple Media, 2003.

Corrick, James A. *Life Among the Soldiers and Cavalry.* San Diego: Lucent Books, 2000.

Grabowski, Patricia A. *Robert E. Lee: Confederate General.* Philadelphia: Chelsea House Publishers, 2000.

King, David C. *Robert E. Lee.* Woodbridge, Conn.: Blackbirch Press, 2001.

McGowan, Toni. *The Surrender at Appomattox.* New York: Children's Press, 2004.

Ransom, Candice F. *Robert E. Lee.* Minneapolis: Lerner Publications, 2005.

Smolinski, Diane. *Soldiers of the Civil War.* Chicago: Heinemann Library, 2001.

On the Web

For more information on *Robert E. Lee*, use FactHound to track down Web sites related to this book.

1. Go to *www.facthound.com*
2. Type in a search word related to this book or this book ID: 0756508215
3. Click on the *Fetch It* button.

FactHound will find the best Web sites for you.

Historic Sites

Lee Chapel and Museum
Washington and Lee University Lexington, Virginia 24450
540/458-8768
To view Lee's tombstone

Arlington House, The Robert E. Lee Memorial
George Washington Memorial Parkway
Turkey Run Park
McLean, VA 22101
703/235-1530
To tour Lee's house and plantation

abolitionists
people who worked to get rid of slavery

annex
to take over a territory and add it to a country or state

cavalry
soldiers who ride horses

Confederacy
the Southern states that fought against the
Northern states in the Civil War; also called the
Confederate States of America

inauguration
a ceremony at which a president is sworn into office

memoirs
written memories from a person's life

pardon
act that forgives a crime

patriots
people who love their country and support it

rebels
soldiers of the Confederate Army during the
Civil War

regiment
a military group made up of several battalions

secede
to formally withdraw from

siege
an operation where an army surrounds a place to
force surrender

Union
the Northern states that fought against the
Southern states in the Civil War

Chapter 1

Page 12, line 6: Freeman, Douglas Southall. *R. E. Lee: A Biography*. New York: Charles Scribner's Sons, 1934, vol. 1, p. 635.

Page 15, line 4: "Resignation Letter to General Scott—Robert E. Lee." American Civil War Portal. http://www.americancivilwar.info/pages/lee/_resignation.asp

Chapter 3

Page 24, line 7: Freeman, Douglas Southall. *R. E. Lee: A Biography*. New York: Charles Scribner's Sons, 1934, vol. 1, p. 47.

Page 27, line 1: Freeman, Douglas Southall. *Lee of Virginia*. New York: Charles Scribner's Sons, 1958, pp. 15-16.

Page 29, line 16: "Robert E. Lee Quotes." *Son of the South*. Robert E. Lee Historical Preservation Initiative. http://www.sonofthesouth.net/leefoundation/Notable%20Lee%20Quotes.htm

Chapter 4

Page 33, line 3: Freeman, Douglas Southall. *R. E. Lee: A Biography*. New York: Charles Scribner's Sons, 1934, vol. 1, p. 117.

Page 34, line 20: Ibid., vol. 1, p. 137.

Page 36, line 1: Lee, Captain Robert E. (His Son). *Recollections and Letters of General Robert E. Lee*. Secaucus, N. J.: Blue and Grey Press, p. 301.

Page 38, line 1: Freeman, Douglas Southall. *R. E. Lee: A Biography*. New York: Charles Scribner's Sons, 1934, vol. 1, p. 190.

Page 43, line 10: Eicher, David J. *Robert E. Lee: A Life Portrait*. Dallas, TX: Taylor Publishing Company, 1997, p. 2.

Chapter 5

page 46, line 1: Lee, Captain Robert E. (His Son). *Recollections and Letters of General Robert E. Lee*. Secaucus, N. J.: Blue and Grey Press, p. 17.

Chapter 6

Page 57, line 18: Ibid., pp. 25-26.

Page 59, line 9: Taylor, Walter. *General Lee: His Campaigns in Virginia, 1861-65*. Dayton, OH: Morningside Bookshop, 1975, pp. 21-22.

Chapter 7

Page 69, line 11: Lee, Robert E. "Letter to Jefferson Davis, Dranesville, Virginia, September 3, 1862." *The Wartime Papers of R. E. Lee*. Ed. Clifford Dowdey. New York: Bramhall House, 1961, p. 293.

Page 71, line 9: Lee, Captain Robert E. (His Son). *Recollections and Letters of General Robert E. Lee*. Secaucus, N. J.: Blue and Grey Press, p. 80.

Chapter 8

Page 73, line 7: "Fredericksburg." *The History Place*. The U. S. Civil War, 1861-1865. http://www.historyplace.com/civilwar/#fredericks.

Page 73, line 10: Freeman, Douglas Southall. *R. E. Lee: A Biography*. New York: Charles Scribner's Sons, 1934, vol. 2, p. 462.

Page 75, line 1: "Thomas J. ("Stonewall") Jackson, 1824-1863." *U. S. History.com*. http://www.u-s-history.com/pages/h399.html.

Page 77, line 3: Freeman, Douglas Southall. *R. E. Lee: A Biography*. New York: Charles Scribner's Sons, 1934, vol. 3, p. 130.

Page 79, line 1: Ibid., vol. 3, p. 157.

Chapter 9

Page 85, line 1: "Appomattox Court House, Virginia: General Robert E. Lee Surrenders to General Ulysses S. Grant, April 9, 1865." *AmericanCivilWar.com*. http://americancivilwar.com/appo.html.

Page 90, sidebar: Redmond, Louis. "He Lost a War and Won Immortality." *American Heritage Library*. http://www.constitutional.net/021.html.

Blount, Roy. *Robert E. Lee: A Penguin Life*. New York: Penguin Books, 2003.

Brother Against Brother: The War Begins. Alexandria, Va.: Time Life Books, 1983.

Constable, George (Ed.). *Lee Takes Command: From Seven Days to Second Bull Run*. Alexandria, Va.: Time Life Books, 1984.

Davis, Burke. *Gray Fox: Robert E. Lee and the Civil War*. New York: Fairfax Press, 1981.

Davis, Kenneth C. *Don't Know Much About the Civil War*. New York: William Morrow, 1996.

Dickson, Keith D. *The Civil War For Dummies*. Indianapolis: IDG Books Worldwide, 2001.

Dowdey, Clifford. *Lee*. Boston: Little Brown and Company, 1965.

Eicher, David J. *Robert E. Lee: A Life Portrait*. Dallas: Taylor Publishing Company, 1997.

Fellman, Michael. *The Making of Robert E. Lee*. New York: Random House, 2000.

Freeman, Douglas Southall. *Lee of Virginia*. New York: Charles Scribner's Sons, 1958.

Lee, Robert E. (Captain). *Robert E. Lee: Recollections and Letters*. Secaucus, N.J.: Blue and Gray Press. {No copyright date}

"Making Sense of Robert E. Lee." Roy Blount, Jr. Smithsonian, July 2003. Pp. 58–65.

Nolan, Alan T. *Lee Considered: General Robert E. Lee and Civil War History*. Chapel Hill, N.C.: The University of North Carolina Press, 1991.

The Robert E. Lee Papers. http://miley.wlu.edu/LeePapers

Thomas, Emory M. *Robert E. Lee: A Biography*. New York: Norton, 1995.

Woodward, C. V. *Mary Chesnut's Civil War*. New Haven, Conn.: Yale University Press, 1981.

Jennifer Blizin Gillis writes poetry and nonfiction books for children. She first became interested in the Civil War while living near Fredericksburg, Virginia, close to many battlefields. She lives on a former dairy farm in Pittsboro, North Carolina, with her husband, a dog, and a cat.

Image Credits